Odd Behaviour
New Poems

Paul Birtill

Hearing Eye

HEARING EYE
TORRIANO MEETING HOUSE
POETRY PAMPHLET SERIES No. 38

Hearing Eye
Box 1, 99 Torriano Avenue
London NW5 2RX, UK
email: hearing_eye@torriano.org
www.torriano.org

Acknowledgements
Some of these poems first appeared in the Hearing Eye anthology: *In the Company of Poets*, in the Apples and Snakes anthology: *Velocity*, and in *Rising*.

 This publication has been made possible with
the financial support of Arts Council England

Printed by Catford Print Centre

Design by Martin Parker

Photograph by Susan Johns

Contents

Watching the Box

It's not dying I so much mind
but everyone watching the box –
my box – staring, imagining –
recalling their own particular
moments with me, and me not being
able to communicate, rest or even
die with such a concentrated force
of eyes watching me. And at the burial
too – all eyes on me again – then the
wake – everyone talking about me and
in my flat – is there no peace?
No, I'll have to wait until they spout
that famous cliché life goes on, and
then forget about me.

Odd Behaviour

Just recently I've taken to putting
up two fingers at funeral cortèges,
and have been beaten up several times.
My Psychiatrist tells me it's just a
phase I'm going through – a kind of
mid-life crisis, not unusual for a
man of my age and background. I asked
him was it common, and he said in some
parts of India it occurs quite a lot
and referred me to the School of Tropical
Medicine.

Four Times a Year

It's always the same
Man drowns trying to save dog
Siege in East London
Travel chaos
Girl abducted
Just another Bank Holiday.

Period

How strange to see Victorians
in old photographs in the prime
of life, walking around with
such confidence and self-assurance,
sometimes with their children,
who are also dead.

First Love

Laughing bathing exercising
    clean underwear.

Checks his bank balance
tries for promotion
buys a jacket
washes his car.

Shows off, tells lies,
distrusts his mates,
thinks about his dead mother
kids, log fires, growing old together.

Stops getting drunk
goes to church
more exercises
more baths
Fresh jokes and confectionery.

Takes her to family home
shows her his old bedroom,
old toys, first school book,
Park where he played
hundreds of snaps and
    Mother's grave.

Strolls around the neighbourhood
holding her hand for all to see

What a find – an acquisition
Mine all mine aren't I clever.

Discovers she's a lesbian
never thought to ask
reverts to a four year old
Stamps his feet, yells
hits her, digs up his mother's
grave and sends her the bones.

Spotted

Drinking alone in my local pub
it's only when the upper deck
of a passing bus peer in at me
that I realize I'm having a shit time.

Fat Misogynist

None of my mates ring me anymore
because they all have girl-friends.
If you can't beat them join them,
but I can't beat them and I certainly
can't join them.

Forty-Three

Yesterday I turned forty-three
and told a friend I'd outlived
Elvis Presley. He said I might
have outlived him in years,
but I certainly hadn't outlived him.
I went to bed early with a cup of cocoa.

Summer-time Blues

It's here again, hot weather and flies,
long days, another football tournament
– how I hate it.

Picnics in the park, men with no shirts on
exposing sickly white skin – everyone wearing
stupid bright shorts.

Kids running amok in beer gardens,
fear of swallowing a wasp, pressure
to go on holiday – sweating like a pig.

Stinking tennis, noisy transistors,
weird things growing, not enough darkness
– talking shit at barbecues.

Laughing couples holding hands, old people
moaning, can't sleep at night and to round
it all off that three day nightmare – The
Notting Hill Carnival.

I don't think I can take another one of these
– let me die in March please.

Grotesque

All's fair in Love and War
I wonder what twat invented
                        this Law.

Perfect Revenge

Although he was very experienced in First Aid
and knew the Heimlich Technique very well,
he still refused to perform the manoeuvre
when his old Headmaster began choking
on a piece of meat at their annual reunion dinner.
He later explained to the Police that he quite
simply didn't like the guy – no charges were brought.

Too Many Hours in the Day

What if the average time spent sleeping
was eighteen hours – people might be
less ill-tempered and happier – six hours
of life is quite enough, though not
much would get done I suspect – but who cares.

The Past

I always prefer the past –
last year, last month,
last week, yesterday,
five minutes ago.
The past is a safer place
to be – to hang out in;
and you don't die.

Why I Never Wear
A Red Poppy

Men love to fight
Men like action
half of them lied
about their age to get in
and loved every moment of it –
best years of their lives –
the camaraderie, adventure,
heroic letters to their girls back home
not to mention the killing.
Men will always fight – in pubs
at football matches – beat up
their wives and children,
and that's why I never wear
a red poppy in November –
it just encourages them.

Courting At Last

This morning I woke up to
the sound of heavy breathing
and thought that I'd finally
scored, but it was a dying pigeon
the cat had brought in.

Behind Closed Doors

I've started a graffiti war in the toilet
of my local pub. It began innocently enough
with a short political statement, but now
it's turned quite unpleasant. Several people
appear to be involved judging by the different
handwriting and various threats have been made,
as well as an insulting drawing of myself depicting
me as a Snake. The Landlady has tried painting
it over a couple of times, but it just starts up again
with increasing nastiness. She's now thinking of
bringing the Police in, as the atmosphere in the pub
is quite tense.

The Big Stink

If only shit was pink
and smelt of roses –
I might be tempted to shag folk,
and I'd certainly enjoy my food more.

Hardly Worth The Trouble

Hitler boasted of creating a thousand year Reich,
instead it only lasted twelve, one more year than
Margaret Thatcher. It wouldn't have sounded the
same at those mass rallies if he'd gone on about
a twelve year Reich, people wouldn't have been
impressed at all – they would have laughed,
and gone home.

2/8/12.15pm Can You Help?

The street is quiet again now,
the morbid onlookers have gone
about their business. The wreckage
cleared – the blood cleaned up –
the motorcyclist dead. A young
couple kiss near the tragic spot
unaware of the fatal accident which
occurred earlier. The icecream man
arrives, but no-one leaves their
house to buy one – it is a hot day
and he can't understand why. In
another part of the city a police
car moves slowly up the road of
the deceased man's parents.

Pigs Liver

Last week I went to my first barbecue
and brought liver. The host was very angry
and said 'What kind of nut brings stinking
bloody liver to a barbecue?' 'A poor and
inexperienced one' I replied.

Empathy

He suddenly realized
what it was like to
feel like everyone else
and consequently felt like nobody.

Fed up

He committed suicide at four
hung himself from his bedroom door
couldn't take any more
done four.

Turn-off

I'd prefer to meddle
with an old car than
unfasten a woman's bra.

In the Kingdom of the Blind
the One-eyed Man Rules

The handsome young but hopeless
alcoholic goes out with the ageing
ex-beauty queen.
The academic professor with club foot
goes out with the uneducated teenage beauty with child.
The obese kind middle-aged man
goes out with the schizophrenic
with big tits.
The pathetic idiot with stutter
goes out with the dowdy bore
with demanding mother.
The rich gay pensioner
goes out with the criminal
athletic black man.
The up and coming young playwright
goes out with his ageing but helpful
literary agent.
The phoney mystic with personality
problems goes out with the impressionable
young drug addict.
The good looking but work shy dope
goes out with the manipulative career
woman and minds the kids.
Occasionally however some people
are lucky and manage to transcend
the barriers of social Darwinism

like the ugly and spotty working-class
labourer who marries the beautiful
daughter of a diplomat and inherits
a fortune.

Paranoid

He checked every new book
of poetry that came out
and every magazine to see
if anyone had stolen his poems.
He was obsessed with plagiarism,
then someone mentioned translations –
what about translations? and unable
to cope with the idea drove his
bubble car over a cliff.

Scary

I remember as a child
being stung by a wasp
my father looked at his
watch and said I could
be dead within the hour.

I remember as a child
falling into some nettles
my father looked at his
watch and said I could
be dead within the hour.

I remember as a child
swallowing some bleach
my father looked at his
watch and said I could
be dead within the hour.

I remember as a child
having a temperature
of one hundred and three
my father looked at his
watch said he was a bit
slow but I'd probably
be dead within the hour.

Benefit King

When I grow up I'm going to be
an astronaut a footballer a physicist
or be long term unemployed.

When I grow up I'm going to be
a rock star an actor a politician
or be long term unemployed.

When I grow up I'm going to be
a doctor a lawyer a fireman
or be long term unemployed.

When I grow up I'm going to be
an architect a marine biologist a painter
or be long term unemployed.

When I grow up I'm going to climb
Mt Everest invent things run my own business
or be long term unemployed.

When I grow up I'm going to have a beautiful wife
three lovely children a big house and flash car
or be long term unemployed.

Near Life Experience

I stopped keeping a diary
it was getting embarrassing
I had nothing to write about
and somebody might have found it.

Span

Man born of Woman
has but a short time to live
but it's getting longer
                    unfortunately.

No. 38

AUTHORS IN THE TORRIANO MEETING HOUSE POETRY PAMPHLET SERIES (in order of publication)

A.C. Jacobs   Jane Duran   E.A. Markham   Brian Docherty   Dinah Livingstone
Adam Johnson   Anthony Edkins   Sue Hubbard   Katherine Gallagher   Kathleen McPhilemy
Simon Darragh   David Kuhrt   Jeremy Reed   Jeanette Ju-pierre   Fatma Durmush
Amanda Eason   Gerda Mayer   Sarah Lawson   Paul Wright   Paul Birtill   Nick Orengo
Dubravka Velasevic   John Rety   Alan Chambers   Peter Phillips   Rosemary Norman
Veronica Rospigliosi   Mario Petrucci   Jane Elder   Beata Duncan   David Floyd   Jo Roach
Florence Elon   Valeria Melchioretto   Sarah Lawson   Sara Boyes   **Paul Birtill**

Paul Birtill was born in Liverpool in 1960, but
now lives in London. This is his sixth collection of
poetry. He also writes plays, three of which have
been staged at Pentameters Theatre, Hampstead.
'Squalor' which was short-listed for the prestigious
Verity Bargate Award, 'The Lodger' which was
Time Out's critic's choice and 'Happy Christmas' is
their current production.

ISBN: 1870841 51 4

HEARING EYE

For a copy of the Hearing Eye catalogue please send an SAE to:
Hearing Eye, Box 1, 99 Torriano Avenue, London NW5 2RX, UK

ISBN: 1870841 51 4

9 781870 841511

£3.00